As A Man Saveth (Heal Your World)

Also by Laban T. M'mbololo, Esq.

Influence: The Secret of Selling

As A Man Saveth *(Heal Your World)*

30 Days of Entrepreneurs' Series

Why are Dumb People RICHER than You?

Fresh Start-off: The Great Themes of Scripture

Influence: The Secret of Management

Laban T. M'mbololo, Esq.@Management for Results

Everything Revealed in the New Management World

Manage by Secrecy: The Hidden Key to True Leadership

Laban T. M'mbololo, Esq. @Selling for Results

Principles of the Top 1% High Performing Salespeople

Great Moments in Sales

The #1 Great Awakening & Future of Real Estate

Beyond The Great Illusion: 7 Sign's you're in a Toxic Relationship

How to Break the Bondage of Prayerlessness

Build a Great Future through Mastering your Mind

The Transparent Leader: First Client Meetings & Negotiation Tactics

The Key to Great Sales Success

The Deal was Great But…

FOCUS (**F**ollow **O**ne **C**ourse **U**ntil **S**uccessful)

As A Man Saveth (Heal Your World)

101 Ways to Save Money and Build a Financial Future

Laban T. M'mbololo, Esq.

Copyright © 2019 by Laban T. M'mbololo, Esq.

ISBN: Softcover   978-1-7960-5108-7
          eBook   978-1-7960-5107-0

All rights reserved. No part of this book may be reproduced or transmitted in any form or by any means, electronic or mechanical, including photocopying, recording, or by any information storage and retrieval system, without permission in writing from the copyright owner.

Any people depicted in stock imagery provided by Getty Images are models, and such images are being used for illustrative purposes only.
Certain stock imagery © Getty Images.

Print information available on the last page.

Rev. date: 10/02/2019

To order additional copies of this book, contact:
Xlibris
1-888-795-4274
www.Xlibris.com
Orders@Xlibris.com
800735

Contents

About the Author vii
Acknowledgements ix
Dedication xi
Introduction xiii
Prologue xv

PART ONE

Character 1

PART TWO

Self-discipline 11
Financial planning 23
Savings Culture 28
Saving Methodologies 30
Multiple Sources of Income (MSI) 41
Effects of saving on; 45
   - Individuals 45
   - An Economy 46

PART THREE

Pension plan and Providers 51

Epilogue 55

ABOUT THE AUTHOR

Laban T. M'mbololo, Esq. comes with a strong academic background with accreditations from the London School of Business and Finance, ASET, Oxford and Cambridge RSA – London, U.K. and stinted World-Class Leadership. International Financial Management, Banking, Forex Trading, Offshore Financing and Real Estate as well as Cross-Border Sourcing –All these frontiers created his desire to explore and transcend beyond Kenyan borders on a learning expedition in the U.S.A, U.K, U.A.E and China to transform his vision in tandem with international standards and best practices. He has also participated in *"Unleash the Power Within"* a very powerful and life changing seminar by Tony Robbins and attended peak performance coaching by Jean-Pierre De Villiers a London based international speaker and best-selling author.

M'mbololo has over 20 years' stint in Word-Class Management, 10 years International project experience, solid Blue-Chip corporate experience with a British multinational financial services company and a pan-African banking conglomerate and is an expert in Islamic Sharia-Compliant financing.

M'mbololo delights with radiating energy in helping people experience a more meaningful and rewarding life out of the works of their own hands and resulting from a complete transformation in their perceptions which accords him a great sense of self-worth with deep expressions of zest for life. The profound teachings of this book constitute a Herculean quantum leap forward in attaining financial freedom that will allow you to laugh much and often, to earn the adoration of intellectual people, the endearment and affinity of children, to treasure beauty, to leave the world a better place than you found it, to realize even a single soul gasped air more easily because of your sheer existence, this is what I call *success*.

M'mbololo has been on National TV to talk on varied topics and also speaks on **10X** Sales Growth, INFLUENCE Sales, World-Class Leadership, Personal Power, Success Principles and Human Capital topics to audiences in the private and public sectors and lectures at the Bandari Maritime Academy on Entrepreneurship. He is also the author of the below best-seller book titles – *Influence: The Secret of Selling, 30 Days of Entrepreneurs' Series & Why are Dumb People RICHER than You? and 16 other book titles.*

ACKNOWLEDGEMENTS

Great appreciation to the authors before me and some of their literature that has remained indelible in my mind and been my driving force towards distilling these wonderful ideas into pearls, you are awesome men and women.

Having previously written a book on sales, I also decided to commit to paper the essentials of money-saving, the most dreaded and least carried out activity by most people in the world, and every reason to address it and embed in a culture which will undoubtedly not only address a rainy day, but will also secure your twilight years and also form a source of passive income and earn you some quiet interest or profit from financial institutions.

DEDICATION

As always, Toni P. M'mbololo, My Dad – a Father with awe-inspiring skill and unsurpassed integrity, a dependable parent, the best Dad ever, this one's for you.

It's a privilege to grow up in a distinguished family where we were always showered with utmost love, never lacked anything and were inspired to take up challenges. You are an adored friend, a real mensch without whose good enlightenment, sheer wise counsel, and willingness to tolerate the intolerable demands of our time growing up, combined with your unwavering support, made this book not only possible but also a thrilling and exciting experience, my lion share of gratitude goes out to you. I'm grateful for even when times got harder you still found a reason to believe in my cause and rally your support behind me; you are awesome and invaluable to say the least.

INTRODUCTION

Building a financial future – the underlying common denominator whether it's achieving your personal goals, fending for your family's future needs, eyeing that parliamentary seat, entering the senatorial or gubernatorial race or even if it's just planning to achieve a comfortable retirement, buying that dream farm house or acquiring a pick-up truck – it all begins with Savings.

Savings is the bedrock underlying the achievement of financial freedom and independence as well as realization of life's goals.

Most households either know the methodologies available for mobilizing savings or get carried away with the hurly-burly of life or indulge in whimsical spending, thereby choosing to be faced with the guilt, grief and fear of tackling the sunset years without a substantial accumulation from a solid savings plan or at least even setting aside an emergency kitty of some sort.

Savings is not only looking for the most discounts and bargains while making purchases, it also entails deliberately setting aside money for a rainy day and the ability to afford a comfortable life after leaving service. Most prosperous people or at least 94 per cent of them, save up to 20 per cent of their annual income and about two-thirds are very conscious about their spending patterns and who in most cases, prefer to acquire very high quality products and services, but at very affordable prices.

The reasons behind establishing savings therefore, are to take care of eventualities and unforeseen contingencies later in life. For instance, it would be prudent to mobilize an equivalent of *six*-month' worth of savings that will keep you afloat, enable you to survive and still maintain the same standards of living and ensure regular payment of bills that never seem to go away even when faced with the wrath of a job loss.

The easiest, effective and most ignored ways of accumulating savings is through change of habits and lifestyle, finding ways to lower the cost of everyday living while still deriving the pleasure from life within your new-found lifestyle. All this is possible, through lifestyle adjustments that are not too frightening and which most households are reluctant to adopt such as – analyzing expenditure against budgets, setting up savings accounts linked to your salary account which automatically debits the funds on pay-day thereby curtailing on any inherent wasteful spending habits.

I vividly remember my Economics teacher at undergraduate level insisting on mobilizing savings if anyone ever had the dreams and hope of making future investment(s) and illustrating this simple principle using an Economics equation: **S=I**; i.e. *Savings* is equal to *Investments*.

The truth of the matter is such that, unless the current pattern of spending and habits change for the better, then your life-goals and objectives will be delusional and therefore difficult to attain. With the new revelations set out herein, I hope it will dispel your doubts why it will not hurt to save towards this noble edifice of building a stable financial future in *101 ways* that I have distilled into a gem of this book.

PROLOGUE

While a lot of literature has been written on how and why to be savvy and mobilize savings for a rainy day is weighty and therefore a matter of life-and-death decision, most authors have overlooked the personal attributes of a prudent saver and every reason that this book in its *Part I* will address habits that inculcate a savings culture which is the cornerstone of any successful savings plan.

Its human nature to sometimes fall off the wagon as saving is one of the hardest things to do on a consistent basis. A large percentage of people don't have any money set aside for emergencies at all, and according to a survey by *GoBankingRates* 57 per cent of Americans have less than $1,000 in savings, 39 per cent of who admittedly accepted to not even having a savings account in the first place.

Since I'm Kenyan, the home of long distance runners, allow me to use some examples of marathoners to drive my points home. Research from Boise State University reveals that ultra-marathoners who are considered brute and beasts, wake up as early as 4:00AM to practically begin their early morning runs, racing a hundred miles or more participating in footraces lengthier than the conventional marathon, are not only good at getting in tip-top condition. They also have a great attribute of controlling finances very well, and as such the research portrayed them to be "financially conscious."

Your reaction may be that, the fact they partake in running all day doesn't avail time for them to spend the money after all! This is further from the truth;

the art of good financial management is permeated by the athlete's mental firmness. Indeed they are hardworking and very goal-oriented both which are great attributes of mega-savers.

Part II will look at the habits and saving methodologies that win the day! And *Part III* will look at retirement and pension plans that work.

PART ONE
Personal Attributes

101 Ways to Save Money and Build a Financial Future

CHARACTER:

1. Keep Your Promises

Tiny fissures evolve as a result of broken promises. Long-distance runners are very much aware of this fact and therefore take it upon themselves to fulfill their promises. Intricate planning goes into organizing a marathon event due to the complexities that arise out of budget and travel constraints. So when a contender decides to sign up for an event or accept donations from well-wishers, in essence they are making an unrelenting promise that they will not only train, but will also beyond a shadow of doubt cross the finishing line. Just the same way newlyweds with flagrant and unflinching love promise the world to each other, it also has a way of ensuring they keep their promises and in so doing this, keeps their marriage intact.

Just Exactly How Does This Work Out?

You are more likely to be motivated when working towards fulfilling certain promises. Staying motivated is what provides the driving thrust to begin making things happen. The moment these goals are put in writing, you essentially have made a promise to accomplish the mission and more importantly reaching your own financial finish line.

Promises are one of the most important tools that help build a foundation of trust to maintain and navigate financial futures. It is therefore important to note that, when you break promises the consequences extend and impact negatively on your future desired amount of savings.

2. Stress Less

Research has shown that runners are least likely to suffer stress, anxiety and experience deceleration in the ageing process. And you guessed it right! Running boosts your self-esteem. The *Financial Health Barometer* research which is a body instituted to determine the relationship between well-being and finances in Australians, established a solid correlation between savings, health and happiness. In fact, it revealed a consistent saver is twice more likely to say they feel with their lives "completely happy" and that they exhibit "excellent health." Optimistic people are very likely to initiate better financial decisions, mobilize more savings, have less debt and also optimism could do wonders for a dwindling economy.

A study by Columbia University revealed that setting and achieving overarching goals has an influence on the happiness levels and raises your confidence. If you are not an ultra-marathoner, take it upon yourself to run the fastest you have ever had on a 5,000 meters footrace, your self-esteem will heartily thank you!

Women Stress about Money

Stress in *America Survey of 2011*, unveiled that top of the list of what stresses women the most is finances and every effort must be done to conserve it. Financial stress and disagreements seem to be the most cited hurdle that leads couples to marital disharmony and eventually conflicts. According to the *Journal of Financial Planning*, women have reported that income distribution of households has been identified to affect wives' marital happiness among other things. Embark on serious savings as an expert tip to de-stress and salvage your marriage and eventually home.

3. Updated Knowledge Base

The knowledge base of ultra-marathoners is meticulous. They scour research materials on the most current nutrient's and nourishment, practice and muscle recuperation techniques from hard intense running, which brings them nearer to their objectives. Similarly, with savings and investments, the lack of financial knowledge and thorough understanding of the risk and return factors leads to poor investment resolutions.

Don't be in a Haste to Make Financial Decisions

Congratulations! If you're already reading this, it means in essence you are formulating the habit of finding more information. What follows? Make it a norm of slowing down when it comes to making monetary decisions. Have you ever come across this quote; *"Behind every successful man there is a woman?"* Rule of thumb; involve your woman in making and arriving at financial decisions and run family wealth like a partnership or company with directors who make full disclosure to one another, grant access to your partner to scrutinize bank accounts and agree to be grilled over unwarranted expenditure. In fact, women raise more objections than provide solutions and every reason to involve them in financial matters to arrive at sound investment decisions. Chances are you will get a lot of queries and feel as if you are not in control of the finances, but the good news is that you will reap the benefits in the golden years. Seek financial advice of experts as often as possible when making long term decisions.

4. Training for a Savings Culture is Mandatory

Rain or sunshine isn't usually a choice for ultra-marathoners, either way upon waking up they have to grab their pair of trainers and pound the pavement. Super savers behave in a similar fashion even in times of economic depression they will still mobilize savings towards their retirement plan and cut back on other unnecessary expenditure.

How to Get Started!

Setting up an automatic deduction directly routed to your savings account is a good-start. Then make it a norm to significantly contribute to your retirement account on a consistent basis and channel any windfall gains to the account if you want it to experience exponential growth. Make it a habit to have the savings account in a separate bank account if possible without facilities of a debit card, online or mobile money access platforms or with a financial institution with a limited branch network and in some inaccessible part of the town or city that counters your access to the money when you feel the urge to use the funds. This discourages you from utilizing the funds even in case of an emergency. The best part is you won't even miss the money because it would be inaccessible anyway.

The Perfect Balance

Ultra-marathoners make it a point of striking a balance between training and their social life. How do you keep life's demand in balance? It's not enough to always treat yourself to niceties and not maintain a savings account, that's not being fair to yourself and the price to pay is very dear and could translate into an uncomfortable retirement and aggravating circumstances in old age and could even occasion early death as a result of succumbing to the pressures of life and not meeting the money demands of the time.

5. Runners Are Conscientious

Conscientiousness is attributable to traits with strong tendencies inclined towards diligence and reliability – keeping things on-task and on-track. Ultra-marathoners go all-out and manifest strong predisposition in conscientiousness. According to a study by Angela Lee Duckworth a psychologist at the University of Pennsylvania, individuals who are conscientious happen to harness more lifetime earnings and also mobilize higher savings for their retirement. "Conscientious people are reliable, meet deadlines and pay their bills on time." They don't know how to postpone things, what is set to happen has to regardless of the circumstances.

Organize or Agonize

Say it after me: *"I can make myself a more thorough and organized person."* These are beneficial tips necessary to put your finances in order. Create reminders on your calendar as well as on your phone for all pending bills. Take it upon yourself to liquidate all outstanding on your credit card bill as though you are racing to the finishing line. And you could go on a small splurge to reward yourself upon "finishing".

6. Self-Educate and Be Certain to Compute

Quick Test: What would be your typical time per minute, if you covered a 2.5 mile curve two times within 45 minutes? Marathoners undergo this kind of computations on a daily basis, but this doesn't mean you have to be a math genius to achieve your financial objectives! Brain power and wealth are not usually in harmony. Take home from this is to self-enlighten on money matters for better financial management. According to a new study in the United States couples who attain a high count on a numerical quiz command more prosperity in the Middle Ages than those who score lowly on such tests and have more stashed away for their requirements in old age.

Did you know that, if you embarked on a savings mobilization plan of just 10 per cent of your total earnings and become abiding and consistent for the long-haul, perennially putting away $200 alone directly from your monthly payroll at an interest rate of 15 per cent over a 30 years stint will translate into a handsome amount of $1.4 million dollars?

How Compound Interest Works to Grow Your Savings and Investment

First and foremost, pave way for some fundamentals on how compound interest works to generate more returns on your investment and also factor in the effects of inflation. Not being a guru in high school math doesn't mean you can't be financially astute or smart. Do you have a habit of postponing when to critically examine your bank statements and don't know what the expenses relate to and possibly don't even have an idea if someone is pinching your money or not? Maintaining a simple expenditure log that you update daily from your check stub will reveal how much you are spending and the exact categories that top the list. This can be done on an excel spreadsheet, phones nowadays also have wallet applications or you could download one if it doesn't have the app. This makes it easier to reconcile your records when the bank statements arrive and it doesn't take time to trace erroneous entries by banks, credit card companies and other financial institutions. Other computations can tabulate the money growth patterns over a given time span. *(Hint; the correct response is nine minutes per mile, in case you hadn't yet figured this out.)*

7. Delay Gratification

There is no better description of "delayed gratification" than the subject delaying the temptation of an immediate reward for a later bigger or better reward. For example, on the night of your test papers you could choose to revise or watch a movie on that same night. If you put off watching the movie for a later date this could mean garnering a better gratifying reward of excellent school grades as opposed to getting instant gratification from that act of watching the movie and jeopardizing the school grades. Similarly, a whimsical or capricious behavior can also be associated with deficient saving competence which is well illustrated using the below *"Marshmallow Experiment."*

American psychologist and Stanford researcher Walter Mischel demonstrated this experiment in three to five year olds and the revelations have to this date become a vital attribute for *Success in Life, Work and Health*. The researcher gave the children choice of an instant treat of one marshmallow (cookie) or wait for 15 minutes and get two marshmallows (cookies) when he returned to the room. This experiment was intended to gauge the children's propensity to delay gratification.

Mischel made an amazing discovery. Approximately 30 per cent of the children were able to put up with the 15 minutes wait time, while some as soon as the researcher left the room jumped and gobbled down the first marshmallow, while others wobbled, recoiled and charged in their seats as they constrained themselves but ultimately couldn't resist and yielded to the temptation a few minutes later on.

There are plenty more insights to learn from this experiment. If you are still reading, it means you are mastering the art of delayed gratification, good luck in applying it to improve your financial fortunes. The researchers carried out sequel and follow up studies on a number of areas in the children over a 40 years span. What was revealed was astonishing. The group that waited patiently for the second marshmallow attained higher SAT scores, experienced less chances of substance abuse, had lower body-mass index, improved responses to stress and superior social skills and were generally successful in whatever they were gauged at.

In a nutshell, the experiment confirmed that there are people in desperate search for quick fix solutions to radically change the lives of others who are sorrowful and grieving. What is more frustrating is that it's an attribute of humankind to fall for such outlandish get-rich-quick schemes when the known and proven methods of attaining success are focus, strategy, passion, hard-work and perseverance (delaying gratification). I urge you to be self-disciplined enough to endure the long route and take the action that will unite with success.

Do You Have Problems Delaying Your Gratification? Start TODAY! Here is How to Do It.

If you begin saying NO to little niceties such as sweets, chocolate bars, cigarettes and saving this towards a sumptuous dinner, in actual sense you will be reinforcing your gratification muscles. Then embark on the big expenditure items like impulse shopping and channel all these funds towards your retirement. Setting aside funds for retirement and other larger than life goals is all about delaying immediate gratification. Do away with that cup of coffee today, the everyday candy bar and this could go towards saving for a dream holiday you have never imagined in Kvarner Bay, Croatia; Los Cabos or Cancun, Mexico; Calabria, Italy; Alcudia, Majorca; Dubai, UAE, New York City, Las Vegas or Miami, USA.

PART TWO

Changing Habits, Lifestyles and Secrets of Millionaires

8. Have a Millionaire's Mindset

> *"The beginning of a habit is like an invisible thread, but every time we repeat the act, we strengthen the strand, add to it another filament, until it becomes a great cable and binds us irrevocably in thought and act"*- **Orison Swett Marden**

You turn out to be what you think most of the time. If you envision yourself as wealthy, want to attain your financial goals and live as a millionaire in your old age, the greatest favor you could do yourself is to be habitually possessed with thoughts and actions that have enabled many to become millionaires. One of the thoughts and habits is that of getting ahead in terms of economic independence. This can be achieved through learning and practicing the art of reorganizing your earning ability, investment activities, expenditure and insurances as well as attaining a healthy work-life balance through how you also spend your passive time. This is a certainty that will get you ahead in terms of fulfilling your financial dreams and objectives.

These habits of attaining financial success are learnable; can be practiced and have been used by thousands of people who have achieved results and have eventually become millionaires. They range from the first generation of millionaires in the United States of America who began from scratch with barely anything and hadn't inherited any wealth. There are also those who amassed wealth as a result of attaining good educational qualifications from recognized institutions of higher learning while others were just college drop outs and others hardly even had high school diplomas. Others traveled far and wide and entered the race as disgraced immigrants, but through learning and practicing the habits of millionaires by doing certain things repeatedly over a period of time they eventually achieved the success.

9. Take Charge of Your Financial Well-Being

Consumer Financial Protection Bureau, CFPB has defined financial well-being as how much your financial situation provides you with liberty to take financial alternatives that let you rejoice in a good living.

This also instills the habit of analyzing your earning capability and savings that will have the effect of curtailing on your expenditure so that you work towards paying off existing debts, watching carefully not to take up new debt and deferring or postponing payments and eventually mastering the act and only incurring the necessary expenditures.

In the meantime, this will avail more funds in terms of your disposable income which you could mobilize towards a cushion known as *Savings*. Once a savings of this nature has been established, you have to keep adding on to it so that the account can experience exponential growth. Additions include but are not limited to; windfall gains resulting from fortuitous activities such as;

i) Winning a lottery, unprecedented inheritance of wealth,
ii) Bonus income,
iii) Sale of a house or disposal of household items,
iv) Unexpected income tax refund etc.

Unlike less prosperous and ill-fated individuals who could end up squandering such unexpected gains, it's prudent to channel them appropriately to stimulate growth of the savings account.

10. Rewire Your Brain for Meaningful Life Changes

Incantations have an impact on how you behave and feel. You will struggle to attain your life goals if your self-prophecy or affirmations are filled with disastrous prognosis, self-doubt, indecision, faultfinding and censure.

Your mandate should be to rescind and negate such thought patterns so that savings and accumulation of wealth are associated with feelings of gratification and contentment, while expenditure and anything that results in an outflow of money should be associated with emotions of pain, feelings which successful people can relate to during their quest for wealth.

Moreover, when feelings of contentment become attitudes associated with accumulation and mobilization of savings, the greater the motivation you get to save more and curtail on all unnecessary expenditures. This will shift the focus to wanting to see how much has been garnered at the end of a given period, say a month, per quarter or half-yearly as opposed to worrying feelings of unpaid bills and piling debts that are always screaming for attention.

11. The Secret is Activating the Law of Attraction

Jack Canfield featured prominently and in mammoth proportions is revered for his role in the foundation of the Law of Attraction in the movie, *The Secret*. He has also written extensively about it and happens to be a great believer of this law.

The key ingredient to fully activate the law of attraction is taking ACTION. In my earlier best-selling book, *"Influence: The Secret Of Selling"* I have revealed how taking action unites success and is an attribute that most prosperous people possess and which unproductive and ineffectual people seriously lack and what makes them wallow in life with dismal results.

Have you ever heard of this common adage, "**#1** *Make money,* **#2** *Use the Money to Make More Money,* **#3** *Repeat?*" This is actually very true when it comes to money matters and is the action phase required to activate the Law of Attraction. Once you have mobilized savings and have begun to feel the positive vibes, the endocrine system begins to produce "feel good" emotions which instill some vigor and vitality that begins to pull and allure more money and financial opportunities in your favor.

Your imagination and innermost work (creativity, ingenuity and originality) constitute a fundamental and indispensable part of your success; an hour spent on the innermost work is equivalent to seven hours of action steps taken in the external world. This doesn't mean that once the innermost work is done, the action step wouldn't be necessary. In fact this is the action step that is required to make a great leap forward to transform your visions into reality. The moment you begin to take solid strides towards your life-goals, you will without a shadow of doubt activate the Law of Attraction and attain greater propulsion which will make your achievements realized quicker than if you didn't have your vivid dreams mapped out correctly. However, if you require tangible, unending and perennial success it's always important to strike a balance between the innermost and outermost voyage.

SELF-DISCIPLINE:

The most vital habit associated with success, accomplishment, joy and gaiety is that of self-discipline. Self-discipline is best defined as the capability to take control of yourself, to take the challenge to work hard or behave in a certain way without the need of someone else telling you what to do. Self-control is an answer and precondition to self-mastery, self-government and self-restraint. The act of being self-disciplined means doing what you have decided to do whether you like it or not. The moment positive feelings begin to emanate, the more you begin to feel you are in control of your life.

12. How to Achieve Excellent Performance

A lot of people wonder what it is they need to do to become successful, not knowing that all they need to excel and have all the dreams they have ever imagined lies within themselves.

Successful people today owe their success to an excellent-oriented state of mind. These are manifested in the form of habits which accidentally develop from the time you are an infant and which end up determining 95 per cent of their behavioural patterns.

Be that as it may, you can still learn any skill you desire to achieve your life goals. Observe the people, who make New Year's resolutions to save up some money, quit smoking, join a health club etc. and keep them till the end of the year who though according to Tony Robbins 88 per cent of them fail at their attempts. Learn from their success stories of what they achieved. They took the effort to learn a new skill and put it into practice to work for them. You can also learn the skill and art of mobilizing savings towards building a sound financial future. The repetitiveness of this learned skill is what produces results and differentiates you from the pack.

13. The Benefits of Mastering your Craft

The pursuit of mastery is one of the habits that thrusts people to be prolific and achieve the highest levels of productivity. This comes from the desire to constantly improve at something that matters the most to you. Mastery is what makes people become prominent and exhibit extreme skillfulness in a given field and makes the difference in this mundane world where tasks are either "push-button" (automated) or outsourced.

The pursuit of mastery is not only important in mobilizing savings, but can also be replicated in the context of work and being the dominant force in revitalizing your life that will give you a great sense of accomplishment. Research has also shown that after *five* to *seven* years of determination, diligence, industry and assiduousness on getting yourself better and better you will rise to the peak of your career, will have invested well and mobilized enough savings for a comfortable retirement.

Five to seven years some people retort is a long time but most people are guilty of starting late and wish they could have begun even much earlier. Five to seven years is actually not a long time and this time will pass anyway, so you better be on your way to getting better in the process improving on the quality of your life and life achievements and you will be within the reach of the top tier or 10 per cent of top performers in your field of endeavor. You will be producing great results than ever before and among the most highly paid in your industry and enjoying great results, savings and investments.

Take into account and acknowledge these three concepts that will help in your pursuit of mastery and that will keep your fire of continuous improvement burning.

i) **It's all in your mind**. If you really want it and set your mind to it, you will achieve it.
ii) **It's a matter of effort**. Consciously making effort every day towards your goal is an attribute that makes life worth living and provides an angle of things from a long-term perspective.
iii) **It's Achievable**. Only when your thought pattern has been synchronised towards self-improvement and achieving at your work and life-goals; savings, investments and your legacy.

14. Everyday Reading Can Impact on Your Life, Here is how!

Everyday reading can introduce you to a broad spectrum of things including but not limited to gaining an upper hand understanding of the secular world, providing insight into different cultures and belief systems that could enable you to contribute positively to conversations with people from different walks of life you meet every day.

Major universities award PhD's, which entail compilation of dissertations from extensive reading and analysis of more than 50 books or thereabouts! If you took it upon yourself to read a book every week, in essence you would have finished reading a tome of 50 books in a year thereby earning yourself a pragmatic and very hands-on PhD in your field of endeavor every year – *That's the Imminent Power of Books!*

The other fact is that without a shadow of doubt you become well read, the most enlightened, proficient and an authority in your area of expertise and most probably the most highly paid professional in your industry if you cultivate the attitude of sparing between 30-60 minutes dedicated to daily early morning reading. There is hardly anyone who cannot attest to the success of this relatively simple practice of daily reading which has the potential to revolutionize and metamorphose your world completely.

This calls for self-discipline in sparing time to consciously invest in early morning reading and staying off the television and social media which have been proven to take up your valuable time and not in the most efficient and productive manner. The rewards are deeply personal and gratifying and you will gravitate towards such a time when you will relax and enjoy the fruits of your hard earned labour. Invest in finding out more on the subject of savings and investment and you will be on your way to a great and pleasurable retirement.

15. Brain Power: Why Your Mind needs Positive Energy

"If you feed your mind as often as you feed your stomach, then you'll never have to worry about feeding your stomach or a roof over your head or clothes on your back" - **Albert Einstein**

Did you know that the spoken or written word can directly have effects on the quality of your life?

This is not a very well known-fact and as a result many people do not have much belief in it. If your life is steadily improving it can get even better, you have the right to a prosperous, satisfying and the most terrific life. However, if your life has stagnated and you are not where you were a few years ago, this is a cause for concern. And if your life is deteriorating very fast this means that at the first opportunity you have to do something right away.

It all begins with a shift in your thought patterns and then everything else will shift along with it. Learn to feed the mind with affirmative thoughts, negativity is so infectious and the many people who resort to this unfortunate option never alleviate the challenges they face in life.

You may not be able to solve the existing political stalemate, or even change the current economic crisis; you could not change the weather or forces of nature no matter the amount of wealth you possess or even if you command the greatest infantry and militia on the globe, there is very little you can change. However, you are fully in control of one thing, and through your possession of positive thoughts this can begin to positively revolutionize your world and this is essentially; *The Power of Your Mind.*

Negative thoughts are self-defeating, drain the quality of your life and drift you towards unhappiness, despair and manifest into low spirits and eventually failure.

When you shift your thoughts, your life will transform along with them. You must guard against your mind as it is your most valuable asset and prized possession. Be like a cell-membrane which is only semi-permeable; shun watching divisive politics on television, violent and tragic ending movies. Decline to engage in endless political conversations with empty rhetoric and no headway. Refrain from reading rape, burglaries and armed robbery columns in newspapers. Spend less time on social media. Keep your mind serene, and at all times influenced by the power of positive thinking and stay clear away from the clutter that will clog and poison your mind.

You become what you constantly feed your mind; therefore form the habit of continuously feeding your mind with great articles, audiovisuals on YouTube, audios or audio books and podcasts that will uplift you to an upbeat mood. Engage in affirmative talks with prosperous people who are going places, who can share positive experiences on mobilizing savings and creation of wealth which will undoubtedly reframe your mind-set and radically transform your life.

16. University on Wheels: Continuous Self-Improvement

There is immense power unleashed in listening to auditory communication such as podcasts, audio programs and audio books while driving to work. This is another important habit that you need to develop for the growth-oriented phase and which is considered a major breakthrough in inculcating values in the field of specialization you intend to learn about.

Approximately a couple of hours or more are spent and wasted in traffic jams every morning commuting. If this time is used wisely in self-educating through listening to professional audio material, this can actually translate into an equivalent of formal education in an institution of higher learning within a few months.

This may not make sense, but look at it this way; students spend more than *ten* hours a week attending to university lectures towards attaining the requirement of varied degree programs. What happens during this period? Your guess is as good as mine! You derive almost the same amount of value within your chosen area of specialisation or what you want to learn about listening to the audio programs and audio books as much as you would by attending to lectures.

Another great way to take in advice and good financial content in any field in an enjoyable, informative and efficient way is through listening to podcasts. It doesn't matter whether you are in need of self-improvement, you are in middle level management or are a business magnate, podcasts will help disseminate information as you work out or travel regularly to and from work. You will find the following podcasts very beneficial and which provide essential tips that can make you review your financial objectives and help you ascend to higher altitudes.

i) *So Money* – it features top business moguls making it a favourite if you want to revolutionise your business and soar to greater heights.
ii) *Stacking Benjamin's* – this podcast is more concerned in helping those that need to consolidate their fortunes and build a financial future.
iii) *The Side Hustle Show* – appeals especially to those who want to generate multiple sources of income in addition to their existing primary source of income.
iv) *Radical Personal Finance* – mainly features stories and interviews on people's financial journeys which help you come up with possible ideas and ways to improve your wealth.

v) *Listen Money Matters* – this podcast will make you have a better hand in handling finances than those of our previous generations as it provides great insights through interviews of known financial experts.

17. Decide Your Own Destiny

"The only person you are destined to become is the person you decide to be" - **Ralph Waldo Emerson**

One way of reaching your destiny is by deliberately choosing it. Who you currently are could be as a result of your childhood experiences whereas the person you become rests entirely upon you. Your destiny is not something to joke about, that you just sit back lazing around and wait for it to happen. You determine your own destiny by the conscious affirmative action's you take and by cashing on and utilizing the opportunities that present themselves along the journey of life.

In one of Tony Robbins *"Unleash the Power Within"* seminar that I attended in Teecom-Media City, Dubai, UAE in 2016, he talked about the power of the mind. This is reinforced by incantations we say to ourselves. As a matter of fact, to make a radical shift in your life, it only takes 10 per cent of your conscious mind.

The Subconscious Mind

Though we have two parts of the mind, we are only aware of the conscious mind. When we have to make a decision, we scrutinize the situation, arrive and leap into conclusions, we are in essence using the conscious part of the mind which forms about 10 per cent of our ability to think clearly and act intelligently. So what happens to the other 90 per cent? It's stored in the subconscious mind which caches all your previous experiences and all things you have ever known. It only takes 10 per cent of the conscious mind to jolt the remaining 90 per cent of your subconscious mind into the motion of conviction.

A positive affirmation or incantation is the most powerful message that the conscious mind can pass on to the subconscious mind. Establish the habit of creating vivid, mind-boggling mental images of performing at your peak and having achieved your life goals and objectives; they will be imprinted on the subconscious mind and interpreted as a reality and it will come to pass.

The ideology is that, if you constantly repeat an affirmation or incantation to yourself over and over again, the 10 per cent conscious mind will begin to believe it and will process and communicate it to the 90 per cent of your subconscious mind as the truth and this will help you to condition the mind and belief system and draw you closer towards achieving your goals and objectives.

Every time this mental impression is created on the conscious mind it sends powerful signals to the subconscious mind which activates and triggers-off your innovativeness, cleverness, creativeness and imagination and pushes you to actualize the images in the real world.

Watch your thoughts, they become words;
Watch your words, they become actions;
Watch your actions, they become habits;
Watch your habits, they become character;
Watch your character, for it becomes your destiny." – **Frank Outlaw**

What you are thinking constantly is what you become. It has nothing to do with your past experiences or thought patterns or even your future thoughts that will shape your destiny, it's the conscious thoughts that you process every moment that seal your fate. Therefore, make a resolution to say positive incantations to yourself every moment, because this also determines a large percentage of your emotional feelings. If someone asked you how your day is progressing, instead of giving melancholy and lukewarm responses like, "okay" or "not too bad", respond in the affirmative by saying "OUTSTANDING," you will feel much better and will indeed end up having an outstanding day!

18. Success Secret: Be Inspired to Get Around the Right People

"You can't fly with the eagles if you continue to scratch with the turkeys" – **Zig Ziglar**

About 90 per cent of your success or failure is hinged on the quality of relations you instigate within your personal and business circles. The more positive people you associate yourself with, the faster you will be able to get ahead and attract more success.

The people you spend time with have immense power over who you become and what you do and every reason this choice should be made consciously and with utmost care.

Before you Change the World, Begin with Yourself

Before making the big step to associate yourself with the right people, it's important to take stock and look at yourself inwardly to ascertain;

a) What do you eventually want to become in your life?
b) What people attributes do you want to mirror or follow?
c) What personality traits do you want to distance yourself and stay away from?

Big Decision: Scrutinize Your Associate's

Once you have determined where you want to be, you will need to surround yourself with people that will take you to the next level. Love yourself enough to do an honest assessment of the people who you spend most of your time with and ask these candid questions;

a) Among all my friends who are instrumental in propelling me towards attaining my desired goals and who is pulling me further away?
b) Who bolsters up the urge to realise my dreams and who scornfully laughs at my pursuits, teases and ridicules me at every effort?
c) Spending time with this person, does it allude to joyous moments or is it always a distress call?
d) Whose company would I feel better with and would provide inspiration?

Having established the above, make it a norm to connect with the type of individuals whose company triggers positive vibes and you want to emulate that are pleasant, respectful and admirable. When out on networking or company events, do not just accept to take coffee with whoever is sat next to you, do not dine with the person standing in the sidewalks or alleyway, do not interact and converse with just about anyone. Be diligent and meticulous and clear-cut on the people you will be around as this has a direct impact on your thought patterns; will sway your decisions and how your association with them overall makes you feel are very important facets of the quality of your life and therefore you will want to consider them cautiously.

19. Learn From the Experts: Gaining Insight into Best Practice

Another growth-oriented habit that you should develop as a professional is that of constantly learning. Many experiences can provide refreshed and vital information that will deepen your skills and overall knowledge whether through a seminar, online course, organizing a research or reading a write-up.

Make it your responsibility to look out for these seminars and supplemental training as opposed to expecting the employer to arrange for them or meet the cost because you are in control of your life as well as your personal and professional growth. Your future and ability to gravitate to the most highly paid or the most knowledgeable in your industry is entirely dependent on you and no one else really cares about it. It's up to you.

A good number of people have invested wisely in these seminars. These could take the form of expensive travels to a faraway country to listen to an expert in your industry. For instance, Jim Rohn, Zig Ziglar or Tony Robbins. Some of them have been life changing in the sense that you learn that important specialized knowledge that will save you the many years of toil and that transforms your life completely and transition you permanently from good to great. In my best-selling book *"Influence: The Secret of Selling,"* Chapter 1 covers the immense power affiliated with *specialized knowledge* extensively.

Nevertheless, there is a remarkable difference between assimilating information and putting it into gainful practice. Without implementation of what is learnt from these valuable courses the efforts could run into waste and therefore every reason why you should adopt an execution strategy.

i) **Identify your Key Strengths: Improve your life**
In order to transfer what has been learnt into practical value-addition, it's vital to apply the strengths in completing the tasks with contentment and accomplishment and fit them in your objective of growth.

ii) **Making the Learning stick and Feedback Partner**
Two crucial ingredients of a beneficial learning agenda are feedback and answerability to ensure a flawless implementation of learning.

iii) **Start with "Why"**
With reference to Corporate ROI (Return on Invested Capital) learning that is not put into practical use is a wild-goose chase. There has to be a "why" that forms the basis of what you are learning. Deep significance is what translates learning into action.

iv) **Put It into Practice: How to Implement Your Learning**
Eight per cent of all money earmarked for training goes down the drain if there is no follow-up training. Continuity training programs and sustenance coaching fill this void to ensure employees and organizations cultivate this all important and crucial self-supporting habits.

v) **Create Action Plans to Accomplish Goals**
For transformation to take place by executing learned information, it's mandatory to have an action plan that will establish and sustain

the habit. Daily reviews need to be conducted and synchronised with your overall objective for realization of success.

20. The objective is to become RICH, not to appear rich!

The objective as always is to BECOME RICH, *not to appear rich!*

A lot of people do not become wealthy because they are possessed with being identified with the emblems or signs of wealth and spend way too much money on this cause while they are actually of depreciable value. Their focus is bent more on appearing rich rather than getting rich.

The rich retain wealth because they adopt the spending habits of the poor. They make it a practice to drive in used cars, dress in moderately priced outfits and watches with only a few owning a second home, private jet or yacht. Self-made billionaire Mark Zuckerberg moved from his rental house into a 5,000 square-foot five bedroom house in 2011 – which is considered modest going by the standards of Silicon Valley and is often seen driving a black Acura TSX, valued at about $30,000. They know that you must not spend more than you earn, and therefore live below their means making it a priority to invest the surplus income in building a financial future - Wealth.

Developing a Millionaires Mind-set

Truly wealthy people are focused on financial freedom and are not distracted by adoration and attention seeking that the average person displays. When you are geared towards becoming rich, you will at a later stage without any doubt consume the luxury goods.

Luxurious goods are there to stay and get even better every day with technological advancements. Acquire assets that generate income, get the money and purchase more income generating assets, replicate this process and you are on your way to getting rich. Purchasing dividend earning shares in blue-chip companies and rental income from high ranking locations are good examples of earning assets.

Think in terms of acquiring shares in a company instead of investing in a zero mileage car. While the average person is spending money to sip beer, do the reverse and acquire the stock in the brewery. Instead of owning a collection of designer pairs of shoes buy the ownership shares in the footwear company.

The people who truly become wealthy spend a lot of time thinking and planning their wealth. While the average person closer to month-end averagely spends *three* hours when bills accumulate pondering about their finances, the rich spend *thirty* hours, ten times that amount of time meticulously planning, analysing and thereby making better financial decisions and therefore achieving more desirable and positive outcome.

21. Everyone in a Race Runs: Only One Gets the Prize

We are all in a rat race whether we realize it or not. We are sometimes faced with the wrath of no steady income, accumulating bills and encountering difficulties in putting food on the table etc.

Before escaping the rat race you need to conduct a lifestyle audit and know where to seriously cut back on, so that you can adjust and still continue with your new-found lifestyle in the wake of a new savings regime. You should at least have a minimum of *three* months expenses saved up and put it in an account that you won't touch, to cater for unforeseen eventualities or hard times.

To get ahead of this race you will evidently need to incorporate the habits of daily reading, attendance to seminars and listening to audio programs and podcasts for updated methods that win the day in cutting back on expenditure by making sacrifices and freeing up finances such as:

i) *Loans and Mortgages* – shopping for the best rates and refinance with an interest rate lower than the existing rate, can result in significant savings on interest costs.
ii) *Insurances* – search for bargains and good offers.
iii) *Rent* – rule of thumb; do not pay more than 30 per cent of your gross pay and if it exceeds either cut back on something else or move out to a cheaper location.
iv) *Subscriptions* – cut on most of the subscriptions to magazines and publications, there are plenty of freebies off the internet. Subscribe to free newsfeeds from social media platforms; consume newsletters links and read magazines and newspapers' free of charge for a specific time period by taking advantage of promo codes.
v) *Cable TV and internet* – disconnect the cable and use up the internet to live stream television programs and episodes.

Weird people willingly make sacrifices like not owning a television set while normal people term this as odd and would even consider you as an outcast. The truth is such that the average person who has incorporated long-term learning that promises success in life through the habit of personal and professional improvement always gets ahead of the genius who goes home and watches television every night.

This habit of continuous learning does not only guarantee ordinary people to becoming top performers, it also sows the most important seed of optimism and confidence. This has the effect of instilling enthusiasm, passion and innovation while still leaving you happier as you continue advancing towards realization of your latent and untapped potential to the fullest.

The process of continuous learning opens up doors previously closed, sharpens your intellect, improves your innovativeness, fast tracks the way up on your career ladder and guarantees unending success and provides a major shift from impoverishment to prosperity and opulence.

22. Being Proactive and Taking Initiative

While exhibiting great confidence, ability to take up varied responsibilities and being highly expectant of great things are good attributes, there is one thing that you need to get past that will stop you from getting stuck in a rut and going beyond a newly appointed post university position.

Truth is such that the ability of being proactive and taking initiative to seek opportunities out of your comfort zone is what promotes growth and development and takes you to the next level.

A research conducted by the *American Management Association* confirmed the above hypothesis. It's revealed in a study of two set of managers;

i) the ones who were successful and
ii) the ones whose careers had hit a plateau.

That indeed the ones who experienced career progression and promotions went out of their way and took initiative to get the job done while those who habitually relied on instructions only acted as such, but the notion of taking initiative appeared foreign to them and as a result experienced career stagnation and achieved dismal results.

23. Defeat Procrastination: Take Control of Your Life

Procrastination has been thought of as a negative consequence that constrains our ability to achieve our life goals. However, procrastination may be viewed positively as this is a way-marker that the brain needs additional information to take decisive action.

Instead of viewing procrastination as a problem, this could be the radical shift needed in your thought patterns and a habit to break free from that you require. Think of it as an agitation, alert or warning signal that something is missing and therefore stopping you from get going and get rolling.

For example, what is delaying you from embarking on your savings plan? Why haven't you begun channelling funds towards your retirement benefits? To overcome this you need to scour for more information on the available savings vehicles, then you need to commit to beginning your savings plan. Ask someone to be checking on you as you progress on, stay away from distractions and persist till you attain this goal and always remember to reward yourself for the achievement(s).

23. Positive Mental Attitude (PMA): Recipe for Success

"A positive mental attitude is a must for all who wish to make life pay off on their own terms. Nothing great was ever achieved without a positive mental attitude." – **Napoleon Hill**

Success doesn't happen in a vacuum. There is a simple science towards achieving it and what you are already in possession of – *Your Mind*. The mind is certainly the single most important asset that you can have control over and failure to do so can render it the largest liability that can prove to be your undoing; it's entirely your decision.

If you adopt an optimistic, progressive and forward-looking mentality, your mind will deliver you to the goals you desire but if you let your mind overpower you, it will occasion unwarranted delays, opposition, doubt, indecision and utmost chaos that will deliver you to an un-ending series of failure and disaster.

Taking charge of your mind to embrace the habit of a positive mental attitude (PMA), to a large extent influences the people you interact with, repulses hindrances, attracts opportunities and opens you up to a world of optimum divine, physical and financial success.

Develop the habit of perpetually thinking of the things you want and focus on attaining your desired goals of savings and other areas of life and shun away any negative thoughts that dissuades you from achieving this objective. Optimism is not just good for the mind; it also boosts your immune system, fortifies and strengthens the body against infirmity and makes it recuperate quickly from a state of fatigue.

FINANCIAL PLANNING:

> *"The secret of financial breakthroughs; pay ten percent of any income you receive to God (Tithe) and saving ten percent of your income as a payment to yourself."* – **Lailah Gifty Akita**

24. How to Stay Accountable and Stick to Financial Resolutions

Financial planning is a continuous process to help you in arriving at rational resolutions about money that can help you in achieving your life goals. This process could involve putting wills in place for your family's protection in the event of illness or premature death, a period that they may have to manage through without your earnings. Factoring all these eventualities together and thinking through the different possibilities is what comprises of a financial plan. You can build your own however, if the needs involved are quite intricately interwoven with different dependents and separate maturity plans you may want to involve a financial planner.

Generally, a financial plan is an all-inclusive evaluation of a person's current earnings and projection of their future financial status by using variables such as withdrawal patterns and asset values to predict the future flows of income.

> *"It's not how much money you make, but how much you keep, how hard it works for you, and how many generations you keep it."* – **Robert Kiyosaki**

Establishing a Sound Financial Plan in Six Steps:

25. Establish your Goals in Life – Short Term Goals.

A short term goal is something you want to achieve in the near future which could be today, the coming week, this month or even this year. These are necessary when considering attainment of long term goals as it helps in breaking them down into bits or chunks referred to as milestones. Once attained, it gives a proud feeling of having done something worthwhile yet difficult as you work your way towards achieving the longer term goals. If the gratification of achieving a milestone is too far away, it becomes strenuous to be dedicated and steady to this cause.

26. Short Term Goals

Are achievable within 12 months or less. Examples;

   a) Enrolling in a gym.
   b) Acquisition of new furniture.
   c) Saving $100 every week.
   d) Making 50 phone calls daily between 9:00AM – 6:00PM
   e) Writing your life plans and setting your goals.

27. Medium-Term Goals

These could take between *three* to *ten* years to realize. They bridge the gap and help in transitioning from the daily activities and onto your longer term visions. It entails planning things between now and when you attain your retirement age. They can be easy to put off in place of shorter-term goals, but don't be deceived and jump onto that bandwagon! Take time to think and seek for more information for planning around the medium-term goals. Once you start achieving them, with more focus, persistence and consistency it becomes a clear indication of attainment of the longer-term goals. Some of the examples could be;

   a) Pursue higher education e.g. graduate school.
   b) Begin a second career or learn a new trade.
   c) Budget for a wedding.
   d) Go for a dream holiday.
   e) Buy a house.
   f) Pay off student loan debt.

28. Long-Term Goals

These are things that are achievable in the future and therefore require some thought process, planning and execution. They are usually not achievable within short-time frames of say a month or a year. Long term goals require time, meticulous planning, diligence and hard work. These goals are not easily attainable and call for striking a balance between articulate planning and commitment. Examples:

   a) Becoming a leader in your field of expertise or industry.
   b) Raising a family and getting children.

c) Going abroad.
d) Saving for a financial future.
e) Starting a business.
f) Participating in community service to tackle preventable diseases.

29. Worth of Assets you Own and Liabilities you owe.

This is simply a personal balance sheet (personal net worth) that shows where you are financially at any given time. It is the net figure arrived at by adding up what you own (assets) and subtracting what you owe (liabilities) and gives indication of how rich or poor you are. The main aim should be to increase the assets side in order to achieve your financial objectives and also improve your net worth.

Asset items will include the following except an inheritance not yet received:

a) Cash in hand and in the bank.
b) Real Estate (market value).
c) Motor vehicles (the resale values).
d) Personal property (resale value of furniture and household items, jewellery, gold, silver etc.).
e) Surrender value of life insurance, treasury bills, share securities, mutual funds.

Liabilities are essentially what you are owed and include debts such as car loan, personal loan, credit card or mortgage loan etc.

30. Evaluate your Current Financial Status

How close are you from accomplishing your goals? Upon identification of your goals it's always good to review and consider what personal preferences to go for in terms of available liquidity, risk and the rates of return on offer.

31. Develop a Solid Plan – Establish a Plan/ Guideline for Reaching your Goals and Objectives.

Here are some tips to help you reach your financial goals:

a) *Know your Goal* – You cannot work towards your goals before identifying them and outlining them in order of priority. You cannot hit a target that you do not have.

b) *Establish a Plan and a Related Budget* – Review goals often and look at the income streams and expense items and prioritize how the money will be allocated on a monthly or quarterly basis.

c) *Preserve your Dreams* – Life is unpredictable so set up an emergency kitty or life and disability insurances (social security) to cater for unforeseen contingencies. The lack of which could resort into use of expensive interest on personal loans or credit cards.

d) *Save towards your Financial Future* – Whether it's that dream home, holiday or retirement plan, it will be determined by the amount you set aside for that specific cause.

e) *Take Delight today* – Reaching your dreams and attaining your life goals entails spending finances according to set priorities. Even if you cannot go out for dinner every evening, set some funds aside and splurge once in a while and enjoy the things that matter today.

32. Implement Your Plan and Make it Stick.

Change is always good however, if this facet is not communicated well it's bound to face some resistance. A successful financial plan should take the transformational efforts of an individual and capture not only their minds, but also their hearts to manage finances differently to achieve the desired results. Key factors to consider in financial planning are:

a) **Level of Experience.** If you have a financial background or are familiar with the tools of financial planning, chances are you will go for the more sophisticated models of investing funds wherein forecasts can be done based on the initial amount, consistent contributions, withdrawal intervals and amounts, any charges or deductibles, rate of taxation, markets where the fund is invested is also pegged on the associated risks and rewards.

b) **Age factor.** The younger you are the more amount of risk you will be able to shoulder and probably the more the returns. When nearing the ages of 40, it would be highly unlikely to want to take up so much risk because you also have dependents and probably school going kids as well and would most likely be swamped with commitments.

c) **Earnings Capacity.** The more the income levels, the more risks one is able to take up and consequently the more the returns, *Ceteris Paribas* (all other factors remaining constant).

33. Monitor and Review your Plan

At least make reviews yearly and make adjustments when needed. With time the set of circumstances change. It is therefore good to review and incorporate change of circumstances that could affect the current financial status e.g. getting married or a new child being borne into the family.

SAVINGS CULTURE:

It encompasses reflected thought patterns, behaviors and working methodologies of individuals in a society or organization in terms of consistent habits done over a period of time to set funds aside. This becomes a depicted way of living and consequently turns into a culture.

34. Early Childs School.

Parents and guardians are considered the first teachers to children while at home. If financial awareness is introduced at a very tender age, then chances are, children will receive expert guidance on financial matters and will handle finances well. This is good for a country because children will embrace a savings culture at an early stage and will be able to initiate investments in viable projects and improve on the economy as well as their living standards.

35. Pension and Savings: Making the Right Decision.

According to a study by *LifeSight*, on wealth at work, a large percentage of employees (about 60 per cent) require guidance in the right direction to make decisions on savings and matters pertaining to setting funds aside for pension.

36. Wrong Priorities: Saving for a Holiday vs. Saving for their Pension.

According to the same study by *LifeSight*, it also revealed that 77 per cent of organizations do not have solid plans for lasting and permanent solutions for their employees' pension and as a matter of fact, 38 per cent of the workforce would rather give more importance to saving towards a holiday or a house rather than for pension plans. In a new research *one* out of *three (1/3rd)* youths would also prefer to save towards buying a home over putting money aside for a pension scheme.

37. Why Millennials save for a Vacation and Delay Retirement Savings.

Student loans, inadequate pension provision, less education on pension matters and runaway real estate characterized by uncontrollable increases in house prices is making the current financial plan of millennials a struggle and impairing their financial future. This makes secure retirement that their parents once envisioned only a folk tale, this is a cause for concern for parents as the *Y generation* are not drifting in the right direction. This is also perturbing investors and the financial services industry because the millenials are defying the unwritten rules of the industry by prioritizing short-term expenditure over long-term and lasting savings plans. This disruptive behavior and pattern interrupt is stirring up future financial hardships for them and reshaping the economic landscape.

38. Financial Literacy: Mandatory to Cultivate a Savings Culture.

A poor savings culture can be attributable to lack of the requisite financial skills. Financial literacy delivered to employees at their place of work is quite instrumental in making them appreciate the fundamentals of money management to handle finances better and be able to effectively set and utilize budgets to build a personal financial future. This can be established through a solid savings plan to shoulder short-term, medium-term and long-term saving objectives whether for a holiday, acquisition of your first home or channeled towards your retirement. Here's the principle; a higher savings culture can help in financing much higher levels of investment and bolster economic productivity in the long-haul.

39. Pension Pot Plans and Affordability.

According to a *Hymans Robertson* research, affordability is becoming a burning and topical issue. Nonetheless, the report reveals that for savers to have a comfortable retirement and have enough stashed away during the pensionable years, they will have to set money aside from their earnings over a lifetime. Similar findings from the *Independent Review of Retirement Income (IRRI)* for the UK's Labour Party for the year 2015, indicated that a target of 15 per cent which is about thrice the average savings that was being mobilized at the time, would be sufficient and left to earn until the attainment of 75 years of age to access a comfortable pension pot.

40. Employers Role in Financial Well-being of Employees.

According to Jonathan Watts-Lay a Director at Wealth at Work a provider of financial literacy at the workplace, the employer has a hand in reinforcing the financial welfare of their employees. This can be achieved through empowering their people with knowledge necessary to evaluate their current financial status in line with their future saving goals whether short-term, medium-term or long-term while controlling risk and minimizing tax liability under different financial scenarios.

SAVING METHODOLOGIES:

Keeping fit is not only beneficial to your health but can also attract more wealth through the savings you will be able to muster. Kick start your personal journey towards an improved waistline and better financial management will follow suit.

41. How to Get Physically and Financially Fit.

One of the recent health breakthroughs has been watchful and alert on moderation in your diet by observing the 90 per cent rule; which means maintaining a healthy, clean and balanced diet 90 per cent of the times and leaving 10 per cent headroom for foods that pleasure your soul such as fries, chocolate and cake. Without moderation, it becomes a daunting task to stay off the goodies that delight you. This same principle is applicable to finances. Allow yourself occasional treats but stick to the amount limit you allocate and once you burst the limit, that's it! Whenever you go out, only take with you the amount you require and don't carry any debit or credit cards, you will be tempted to spend slightly more than you had intended. According to a research by *Consumer Expenditure Survey* of 2016, Americans were notorious for having spent an estimated 44 per cent of the allocation for food rations on eating out. Staying within your spending limits is therefore important and a very deliberate and calculated move to keep on track of other expenditures while still setting aside some funds aside for your savings plan.

42. Truth No One Admits but Will Benefit You.

There are body parts that are your weakest link and which you would avoid to train at all costs when you hit the gym, such as forearms and abdominals. Rule of thumb; learn to start with these trouble areas so that when you are done and dusted and the fatigue sets in you don't have to worry about working on them.

Similarly, embark on keeping track of your finances which is an exercise that most people dread. Set aside a day once a week to monitor expenditures through applications such as *Wallet* for iPhone to stay accountable and automate transfers from your checking account into your savings account.

43. Get on The Move.

Adopting a lifestyle change can lead to better health and will also make some money for you. This is a deliberate attempt to coincide frugality (meanness) with passion to keep fit while saving as much as possible. Instead of enrolling in a private members club, join a local gym at a very subsidized rate. Opt for outdoor events such as evening walks, jogging, swimming and bicycle riding which won't cost a pretty penny.

44. Ditch a Bad Habit: Save Money.

Shoot for something that is detrimental to both your health and wallet. Quitting smoking is beneficial to the body and is also friendly to your pocket. Consider this; if you spend $9 dollars on a beer a day, if you decide to quit like cold turkey, this will translate to $3,285 dollars annually. If this will have the effect of reducing your fuel budget of driving around looking for night spots by $150 per month, this will amount to a massive savings of $1,800 per annum. The total works out to $5,085 ($3,285+$1,800) which could be channelled towards your individual retirement benefits account and you will be on your way to a gratifying retirement. Other lifestyle adjustments that could save you lots of dollars include; cutting back on soda, candy bars, chewing gum, seeds and nuts, beef jerky etc.

45. Why You Should Take Advantage of Employee Benefits.

A lot of times employees only take into consideration health benefits offered by the employer, but there are a lot more other fringe benefits that the employer has to offer that you could take advantage of through a close scrutiny of your enrolment or employment terms or letter of offer. This could help you decrease your tax liability and free up some money that will help and can be used to defray your travelling costs, and even pay for crèche or day-care expenses.

46. Brand Loyalty is Not Good for Your Wallet.

Once you realize the amount of savings that you could make by reducing purchase of branded products you will get hooked. Generic items cost much less and most of the times, there is not much of a difference in the quality or taste. You could still stick to some brands which add value, though for the most part do not allow yourself to be a slave to brands, opt for 99 per cent generic items as they are almost the same quality or sometimes even better than trusted brand names and a lot more cheaper.

47. Avoid Taking Credit.

If you currently do not have a job and are not making any money, it is not a good idea to solicit for credit in the form of either loan or credit cards. The odds are such that you cannot curtail on unnecessary expenditure and temptations will be too high and not worth the pain and trouble of repaying such a debt. Such debts should be wisely channelled towards viable projects that can self-sustain with at least a minimum of *six* months assured repayments covered.

48. Stop Eating Out: What Happens?

> *"Don't tell me what you value, show me your budget, and I'll tell you what you value."* – **Joe Biden**

There is nothing as gratifying as grabbing a mouth-watering double cheese burger from McDonald's or a favourite chocolate sundae from KFC. But when you get back home you wonder where all your money went to! Take a moment and scrutinize your budget for eating out, fast foods will probably be the largest expense item.

Plan your meals and be more consistent with grocery purchases. Meal planning is vital to keep the grocery costs low. Do this for 30 days and notice the amount you will save. If it becomes socially boring and gets difficult, take the challenge with like-minded friends and alternate cooking at one another's house instead of splurging on whimsy lunches and dinners.

Make a healthy sandwich, rummage through leftover from dinner and don't be afraid to get creative. To avoid last minute early morning rush; pack your lunch well in advance on the previous night. Even better, it makes you to avoid the urge for spending on lunch.

49. Curtail on Impulse Purchases.

One of the ways of saving money is by cutting back on impulse purchases. Buying on impulse is a big problem because if you see something which is on sale or there is a good offer and there is money in the accounts, chances are you would go for it. This has a negative effect of draining hard earned money from your account which could have been used for other gainful purposes.

Reports from *CNBC.com* reveal that shoppers typically spend about $5,400 annually on impulse purchases. Curtailing on impulse expenditures will save you a lot of your money which can also earn you silent interest sitting in the banks or other financial institutions.

Here is an important discovery, a lot of outfits, footwear and many other artefacts bought on impulse would usually just lie around and hardly get utilized. When you take time to plan your purchases you end up buying the things that you actually need and derive a lot of pleasure and satisfaction from using.

When you intend to buy things, make a note of them and move on. Then later on, get into the habit of doing some homework of finding some bargains and after a wait period of usually about 24 hours or slightly longer, then make the determination if you would still need the item or if it's still helpful.

50. Take Keen Interest on Mortgage Rates.

You should adopt this practice even after buying your home. Chances are that if you don't keep a lookout for such great deals it follows that you could miss out on refinancing options which could tremendously drive down your cost of finance over the repayment period.

51. Adopt the Envelope system and keep Cash to a Minimum.

Cash is powerful and can get you great bargains but will not necessarily solve all your problems however, a plan for the money will. When end month nears, allocate the money according to budgeted categories in separate envelopes such as for clothes, groceries, bill payment, bus fare, lunch etc. and stick to the budgeted amounts.

52. Have an Exit Strategy in your Savings & Investment Plan.

When you don't have one it's hard to pin point where to cut your losses and sell your stock or when to take your profits and move on.

53. Past Performance is Not a Predictor of Future Results.

View every savings and investment goal independently and carefully consider all the factors affecting the outcomes.

54. Maintain a Budget and Adhere to It.

On money matters', failing to plan in most cases is planning to fail, therefore don't draw a budget if you will not have the discipline to follow it to the latter.

55. Maintain your Car: Extend its Lifespan.

Stick to the maintenance schedule of your car it will have a positive effect on the miles per gallon you get. If your budget is tight, consider replacing the air filters, lubricants and oil filters. Regular maintenance not only addresses issues affecting fuel consumption, it also reduces the risk of encountering a major breakdown which could further drain your pockets.

56. Filling at the Bowser: Full Tank vs. Half Tank.

There are many theories on this. Other proponents are of the view that if you fill up the tank it's an extra weight on the car and costs more to carry its own weight. While you will still need to go back to top up if you opted for half tank, whichever school of thought you belong to, it makes more sense to fill up the tank when you have the money and this will save you extra costs of trips to the bowser and prices could also have bounced back up.

57. Change your Driving style.

Many drivers do not notice a correlation between their driving practices and fuel consumption. Avoiding hastened accelerations, rapidly raising your RPM's and following the posted speed limits could prove to be friendly to your pocket.

58. Re-examine your Route.

This applies to the routes you often use to get to work. For instance, if there is a much shorter option but has multiple traffic lights, many road signs, and meanders around hills, you will end up consuming more fuel or gasoline as opposed to using a much longer route with a much levelled road and less stop signs.

59. Pay bills on Time.

We are sometimes not concerned even when we pay bills late. There are a handful of advantages for paying on time such as an improved credit score, eliminate late fees on credit cards and the related finance charges especially on returned checks (cheques). Consider signing up for auto-pay, set up bill payment reminders and where possible consolidate bills.

60. Making Minimum Credit Card payment Each Month.

A lot of credit card companies require a minimum payment usually between $25 to $40 which could be a fixed amount or a percentage of your total outstanding bill. Don't fall for this trap, as you will not only end up paying more but also pay the maximum interest rate. The less you pay now, the more you will pay later and over a longer period of time.

61. Avoid Payday Loans or Loan sharks.

These are loans which are accessible without a credit check and no application process. These loan sharks or payday lenders charge a range of $15 to $30 for every $100 loaned out. Typically, if you borrowed $100 and the lender charged a flat fee of $15 making the repayment would be $115 or 15 per cent. This may appear like 15 per cent but do the Math; this works out to 390 per cent per annum which is exorbitantly higher than the applicable bank or credit card rates. For those who are of the notion that a payday loan will not cause any harm as long as you don't make it a habit, think twice!

62. Expecting an Inheritance? Don't Count on It.

If you have struggled to prosper in your life financially and are waiting for an inheritance from your parents or loved ones to change your financial fortunes or solve your financial quagmire, then that's a bad idea.

Here is why. You may have to wait for them to pass on to get the inheritance. If the parents live longer than was anticipated, their retirement benefits could run out and you could end up supporting them in old age.

63. Boost Your Social Security Retirement Benefits.

Total dependence on Social Security without a separate saving is a big mistake as it was not designed to sustain retirees to the fullest. Most senior retirees will require almost 80 per cent of their previous incomes for a comfortable living in old age to cover all living expenses and also to be able to engage in other leisure activities and pursuits.

64. Buying a Car – New or Used?

The main disadvantage of buying a new car is that you leave 20 to 30 per cent of its value when it drives off the lot. The advantage of buying a used car is that someone else bears the largest depreciation hit on the car which is within the first 2 to 3 years, since this is not an investment.

The insurance rates on a used car will also be considerably low and many reliable makes and models can give mileage of up to 100,000 comfortably or just before they are *ten* years old. Be sure to dispose it off on or about year *eight*, just before it calls for a major service.

Rule of thumb on financing is; you should be able to service and clear the car payments within *thirty-six* months otherwise it means you were not ready for the purchase decision in the first place.

65. Monitor Your Credit Reports.

Stay on top of your credit health by perusing through your credit reports regularly or seek paid-for expert guidance and help. This can help detect any fraudulent activity, sign of identity theft or erroneous entries that could hurt your credit score.

Your credit scores affect your ability to solicit for approval of credit facilities in the form of auto loans, credit cards and personal finances. A lower score also means it's harder to qualify for borrowed facilities and even if you did, it would affect the terms which could be priced higher than the normal interest rates.

66. Prioritize Your Own Retirement over Children's Future.

It's important to ensure that you have secured a great retirement for yourself before saving towards your children's high school or university education. Otherwise what good would it do if you spent your sunset years eating food that the horses feed on?

67. Handle Billing Errors on Your Credit Card Statement.

Make it a habit to regularly review your credit card statements to look out for erroneous entries, unauthorized charges resulting from clerical errors or a credit card charge that has been possibly cleared from the wrong account.

Lifestyles Habits and Secrets of Millionaires You Should Adopt to Build a Financial Future:

68. Have Patience.

Even though you have heard outlandish stories of people becoming millionaires overnight, the typical millionaire takes about *twenty-two* years to make it and would usually be in their *fifty's*.

69. Setting Daily Goals: Achieving Great Success.

Millionaires set daily goals whether they are planning for the week, or considering possible options for multiple streams of income. This helps a lot in keeping their focus and gives them impetus.

When establishing daily goals it's very important to have them in order of priority. This simply means that, in the pursuit of making more money you should embark on activities that will rack you millions rather than chasing those that stream in only a few thousand dollars.

70. How They Avoid Debt.

Millionaires avoid getting into debt at all costs. They have perfected the art of being frugal and will only make purchases that they can cover the cost of with cash. Cash is always preferable to them because it carries a zero per cent interest rate. They would book a holiday and pay for it using a credit card, and clear the whole outstanding bill, thereby avoiding the hefty interest charges.

As a principle, millionaires will only incur and pay using credit cards if they are certain to clear the whole bill when the statement arrives and falls due for settlement.

71. Have a Passion for What They Do.

If you really enjoy and love what you do, it makes it easier to achieve and become a seven figure earner. An example of a seven figure earning ranges from $1,000,000 to $9,999,999 imagine earning this kind of income? Author Tom Corley who has researched widely on millionaire habits sums it very well, "Those people who pursue a dream or a main purpose in life are by far the wealthiest and happiest among us. Because they love what they do for a living, they are happy to devote many hours each day driving towards their purpose"

72. How and Why you should Pick the Right Life Partner.

This is one of the most important decisions that you will have to make in your lifetime and that according to Robin S. Sharma in his book *200 Secrets of Success* will guarantee you 80 per cent of your happiness, success and pillar of support and therefore every reason you should make it wisely. Shared values reinforce the foundation of your relationship. Millionaires find spouses who share in their value for money as well as money spending habits. This attribute alone will make you work as a cross-functional team that makes good decisions in being thrifty and money-saving, day-to-day spending as well as making investments.

73. They Avoid Spendthrift Friends Like the Plague.

One of the distinctive features of millionaires is the wilful and deliberate effort not to hang out with spendthrifts and credit card minions. We pick good and bad habits from friends and our associations. If your friend quits smoking you could find yourself on the verge of stopping and if your colleague began skipping gym sessions to attend parties you could easily follow suit. Money decisions are not an exception to this rule and the reason you need to associate yourself with like-minded people who are frugal in spending and the probable reason that their good money spending habits will transform you into an economic and cost-effective individual.

74. Set Savings Goals at an Early Age.

It can be said that 94 per cent of all self-made millionaires made it a goal to save at least 20 per cent of their net earnings or revenue that they generate. This is often a tendency that they began in their early lives way before they racked their millions.

The whole idea here is to begin the habit of saving some portion of your net earnings even if it is 2, 5, 7 or 10 per cent. Once this saving habit has been established then work hard to at least bring it up to 20 per cent and wisely investing these savings. Brush up for some basics in compound earnings and get the savings to work for you through sound judgement of investment opportunities.

75. Read a Lot.

Prosperous and well-heeled people do not rely on social media feeds on Tweeter, Face book or television for their information. According to author Tom Corley almost about 88 per cent of millionaires spend not less than 30 minutes every day reading for general knowledge, tracking developments in their fields of endeavour where they have vested interests and also read biographies on successful individuals.

76. Value their Health.

Millionaires are generally early risers who are usually up by about 6:00AM in the morning and who averagely get sleep of seven and a half hours. Apart from indulging in regular exercises they also pay close attention to their medical and dental check-ups and make it a tendency not to miss their appointments.

77. Know where to Say NO.

Elliot Herman of *PRW Wealth Management* once said, "In my experience, my wealthiest clients have the ability to say no to people or ideas that they do not understand or lead them off course."

Warren Buffett who is one of the richest men in the world and possesses great business acumen declined to invest in the dot-com companies and the technology bubble burst of the 1990's because he didn't understand them. It became apparent that he was right while the pessimists who termed him both a conservative and old fashioned were not only wrong but also lost their money.

78. Stay Focused and Avoid Distraction.

The wealthy are very keen on achievement of their goals as well as keeping track of where they are. Tom Corley author of *"Rich Habits,"* narrates that about 70 per cent of millionaires will work on at least accomplishing one goal in a year. They would also put in a great deal of time defining their goals and designing the achievement plan, they persevere and stick to it.

79. Who Are the Entrepreneurs?

Adopted from the "Millionaire Next Door"

> *"Twenty per cent of the affluent households in America are headed by retirees. Of the remaining 80 per cent, more than two-thirds are headed by self-employed owners of businesses. In America, fewer than one in five households, or about 18 per cent, is headed by a self-employed business owner or professional. But these self-employed people are four times more likely to be millionaires than those who work for others."* – **Kenneth Blanchard, Ph.D.**

Millionaires appreciate that life is too short and would therefore prefer to do what they love to do most than working for somebody else. There are times when it's quite risky and you sometimes falter, however it pays off both personally and financially.

MULTIPLE SOURCES OF INCOME (MSI):

Want to become a Billionaire? Create Multiple Sources of Income...

> *"There is a difference between interest and commitment. When you're interested in doing something, you do it only when it's a commitment. When you're committed to something, you accept no excuses, only results."* – **Thomas J. Stanley**

80. Why do 1 per cent of the population Control 82 per cent of the Wealth in the World?

According to Tom Corley the top tier 1 per cent will continue to control the worldly wealth up to such a time when the remaining 99 per cent puzzle it out, understand what the 1 per cent are doing and emulate their steps and begin to multiply these efforts.

The affluent know this secret too well and as a result have created Multiple Sources of Income (MSI's) that make them work once and experience continuous streams of income flows over a lifetime and from different sources.

81. Primary Source of Income vs. Multiple Sources of Income

Your primary source of income or PSI is what for the world's population forms about 96 per cent of their major revenue-generating activity which usually is a job. Your PSI is your job.

Problem(s) with your PSI;

- It doesn't pay that much though it does take care of the bills.

- Not much is left even with a well-paying job. You tend to want to go to all the nice places, dress in classy outfits, drive in flashy cars etc.; but when the income stops, the lifestyle is adversely affected and there is nothing else to show for it and you are back again on the rat race. (*Refer to #21 above*).

Any sudden change of circumstances could drastically affect the PSI and will impair the primary source of earning and therefore this becomes a big challenge to rely on for a peace of mind.

82. Alternative Income: Why you need Multiple Sources of Income (MSI's)!

An MSI is not a second job but rather refers to positive inflows of income. When the wealthy become very successful at their PSI, they don't just stop there. They go on to create MSI's which allow them to multiply the primary source of income, replicating the same or similar services and earning multiple times from these activities. This relatively simple concept is what has made wealthy people very successful and what differentiates them from the average person.

A good example is when a real estate developer undertakes to put up *sixteen* semi-detached maisonettes. Upon completion, he may decide to sell *ten* units so that he can clear the debt he incurred towards building the maisonettes and decides to keep *six* units which he then collects rent from. The real estate developer has created positive cash flows from the maisonettes which are liberated and absolutely free from debt.

Another example is publishing a book or magazine. When it's sold over and over again across borders it generates positive flows of income and in essence an MSI has been created. This frees up time to engage in developing other MSI's.

Factors to Consider for Evaluation of Potential MSI's

All wealthy people have chosen the MSI route. I will share some general guidelines to adhere to until such a time that you have established confidence is setting up MSI's and become an expert and gotten a complete hang of it.

83. Adherence to Low-risk

When investing your hard earned money, investments with high returns and considerable low risk are always preferable. Some of the low risk investments would be fixed deposits (certificate of deposits), high interest savings accounts, money market, and treasury inflation insulated securities such as treasury bills, treasury bonds etc.

84. Offer High Returns or are High Yield Investment Options

This is a rule of thumb that; MSI's *must* yield high returns. Look at it this way; there are many ways to make the big bucks, why would you opt for the excruciating slow gains when there are quicker and better methods? Higher yield investments also means dealing with greater risks as there is no free money in this world. Higher returns are associated with high risk therefore be on the watch out, attend and heed to the details and be on the lookout and query anything and everything.

Understand components and features such as cost implications, operational conditions, trade and industry competition and the prevailing market and economic conditions before determining the potential returns.

85. Modest Time Requirement and Participation

Financial success is not hinged on spending lengthy amounts of time on MSI's. In fact MSI's that demand a lot of time involvement and don't guarantee immediate returns tend to be an inhibition and hence the reason why in the very beginning MSI's need be carried out on a part-time justification until the act is fully perfected and they have become self-sustaining.

86. MSI's have to be Distinctive and Extraordinary

The more distinctive MSI's are the better. There is no point of reinventing the wheel. This aspect of the MSI's being distinct may attract investors and other equity partners as they would want to pride themselves with being associated with an exemplary and out of the ordinary money-making venture.

87. Reduced Energy Demands

Experience shows that the more the MSI drains away a big portion of your energy levels, the less motivated you are to pursue it further. Good piece of advice is; either work with ideologies that require less energy or involve others so the task at hand can be broken down and the efforts evenly distributed among the would-be dream team.

88. Require Critical Thinking and Other Higher Order Thinking

MSI's should be based on ideologies and not hard work. Working with details of information on facts and figures is more cost-effective and financially rewarding than working on an excavation site with spades, stonecutters, hammers and chisels.

89. Inexpensive Resource Requirement

This calls for application of the law of leverage. A common delusion is that leverage applies to borrowing finances.
What is leverage? It's simply the capability to influence a lot only with a tiny proportion of a resource.

Forms of Leverage

i) *OPM (Other People's Money)* – allows you to acquire assets quicker and command a large stake than saving such an amount would, as it could take a considerable amount of time and the purchasing power could be eroded by inflation over the years.

ii) *OPT (Other People's Time)* – companies sell their time in the form of specialization taken up by professionals with special skills as well as labourers. Hiring all these professionals such as lawyers, accountants, realtors and actuaries allows utilization of their skills and knowledge while at the same time freeing up time to make additional income from other MSI's.

iii) *OPW (Other People's Work)* – has similarity with OPT but you instead hire people to leverage on their time. Bill Gates applies this principle widely and is able to effectively leverage on time, ability and energy of almost 70,000 employees. This explains why at the end of every year Gates still emerges as *one of the richest men in the world* yet at the beginning of the year we all have a similar allocation of time available which is 8,760 hours or 525,600 minutes in our *time bank*. Gates has perfected the art of utilising OPW to his own credit.

iv) *OPI (Other People's Ideas)* – this alludes to replicating great revenue generating ideas. Businesses utilizing networks and franchises' are existing proof of OPI at work examples are popular restaurant franchises - McDonald's, Subway, Wendy's, Domino's Pizza, Pizza Hut, Burger King or KFC. The basics of wealth creation never change; it rests entirely on leveraging on OPI.

v) *OPE (Other People's Experiences)* - it's a complete waste of time to relearn what other people have known and perfected over the years. The best way to tap into OPE is through learned experiences, expertise, as well as flaws and faults of others. Common examples would take the form of colleges, universities, audios, seminars and podcasts.

EFFECTS OF SAVING ON;

- Individuals

90. Reasons for Savings for Individuals

People mobilize savings for some of the following reasons;

i) To provide for old age security or for future expenditure.
ii) To provide for unforeseen contingencies or for a rainy day.
iii) To leave an inheritance for family or next of kin.
iv) Other reasons;
    a) Change in social status.
    b) Wealth accumulation.

91. Savings Rate

This refers to the amount of money that is deducted from disposable income (what an individual is left with after tax) of an individual's earnings and is directed towards purposes of establishing a retirement plan. The amounts could also be channelled to safe investments in the money market in the form of treasury bills, treasury bonds or securities such as shares and stocks.

92. Savings Rate and Gross Domestic Product, (GDP)

The amount of savings expressed as a percentage of the GDP indicates the monetary state and financial growth of a country. Savings that is mobilized by individuals or households is the major contributor and source of government borrowing. The government creates a public debt by borrowing from the savings of individuals to fund public projects such as roads and bridges or through creation of a common pool of funds for private investments.

EFFECTS OF SAVINGS ON;

- An Economy

93. Savings Rate vs. Economic Growth

The Harrod-Domar model of economic growth postulates that the savings level is a pivotal ingredient in driving growth rates of an economy, though most of the savings rates in Africa are comparatively low at 17 per cent of the gross domestic product (GDP).

In fact, there is a positive correlation in that an increased savings rate means banks are well capitalized and could advance loans at low interest rates for capital investments to;

i) The government.
ii) Private investors.

This also has the effect of increasing the capital stock or shares traded in the stock exchange and an increment in the cash holdings.

Increased savings rates for individuals avails more to the financial institutions to lend more to organizations for enterprise. An economy characterized with low savings means choice of short-term consumption over longer-term goals which could starve the economy of beneficial investments which could lead to shortages and future disadvantages.

94. The Impact of Savings on Economic Growth

How do individuals, organizations and economies increase their riches and wealth? This is accomplished through mobilization of savings and is determined by the following factors;

a) Preference of future consumption as opposed to current consumption.
b) Their income expectations.
c) And to some extent the prevailing interest rates.

As a rule of thumb, curtailing current consumption paves way for investing for the future. It enables acquisition of machinery and equipment for businesses and enterprises while governments are able to invest in medical facilities, schools, better roads and bridges and generally improve the infrastructural facilities all geared towards heightened economic prospects in the future.

Individuals and organizations save and invest when they have trust in the financial institutions that manage their funds as well as having faith in the economy. In the recent past, it was not safe to stash deposits in African banks but a current wave of change has blown which has seen the Central Banks tighten their grip by being more stringent on its mandate on the regulatory framework on financial institutions, only allowing operation of credible commercial banks. According to the *Business Daily* in what has popularly became to be known as "flight to quality" that was catapulted by the collapse of Dubai Bank in August 2015, Imperial Bank in October of the same year and Chase Bank in April 2016 in Kenya that resulted into panic withdrawals from banks considered to be small to relatively larger that were perceived considerably safer banks.

When the aggregated savings of a country increase, this creates a pool of cheap funds available for borrowing by customers in the banks as well as the government.

The higher the savings, the lower the interest rate the banks charge and this spurs economic growth because it attracts investors to borrow for investment purposes in the country. This also creates higher volume of goods and services through increased production which also increases the gross national income figures. This means that there will be higher income levels per person and this will result in increased income for citizens of a country.

Countries in rich economies save more than their counterparts with weaker economies who channel bulk of their income towards immediate consumption. Rich and wealthier nations have a higher composition of retirees who have set funds aside for their sunset years though some poor economies have been able to break from this cycle of high current consumption and low savings and especially in East Asia which has propelled vibrancy in their economic activities. China is a case in point where almost 50 per cent of the production proceeds are channelled towards savings and re-invested back into the economy.

The governments can offer *three* incentives to individuals, companies and itself to tremendously boost the rates of savings as hereunder;

a) *Bolster rights on title ownership in property* – will increase savings and investments of individuals in the real estate industry.

b) *Improvement of the business environment and resolving issues on infrastructural facilities* – will foster investment in energy and transport projects in the sectors and as a result amount to increased savings.

c) *More focus on infrastructural projects* – governments need to curtail on re-current expenditure like salary and wages, goods and services and invest more in long-term projects – better roads, bridges etc.

PART THREE
Savings & Investment Vehicles

PENSION PLAN AND PROVIDERS:

95. Retirement Savings Plan.

This is one of the top benefits that you could derive from an employer. Because everyone needs to save for a retirement, even self-employed persons could take up this savings plan. There are also tax advantages attached for a 401(k) or 403(b) if you are employed or a 401(k) s if self-employed in the US.

The contributions towards these plans are done on a before tax basis and more often than not the employers match your contributions to the scheme. An employer matching your contributions essentially means that is free money up for grabs, my recommendations are; at the least make as much contribution as possible to attract the matching employer contributions. Another benefit is that the earnings on the investment are tax-deferred (not taxed until a later date) until such a time that a withdrawal is made from the retirement benefit.

96. Educational Provider.

There is a variety of savings accounts that are offered by employers that only earmark funds for purposes of college education for your children. The main advantage of these plans is that, funds are recovered automatically from payroll by the employer and before you lay your hands on it. These investments don't have pre-tax benefits however, there are other tax benefits attached to them depending on the different options employers may offer.

97. Medical Provider.

This is an important benefit that needs to be reviewed annually for the following reasons;

a) Your employer may effect some changes to your benefits entitlement.
b) In embracing cost cutting measures, your employer could review your co-payments or deductibles upwards.
c) Possibly changing the medical provider.

Personal circumstances may change along the way; maybe you got married or had additions to the family. The medical provider may have been helpful at the beginning before you bore children and may not now be your best option. It could also be the fact that you are not happy with their referral terms on your existing medical plan or require more expert consultation.

Make it a point to read all the provided information by your benefits administration department before you renew your policy or select another one according to changing circumstances at a given time. It therefore shouldn't be automatically renewable upon expiry of the validity period.

98. Life Insurance.

Suppose sudden death resulted, life insurance wouldn't replace you, but your family will be entitled to a certain amount of monetary value depending on the coverage. If you have school or college going children, the life insurance will ease the financial burden and responsibilities on your spouse towards fees and mortgage repayments.

Companies offer one form of group life insurance or another at discounted rates of premiums. Other company plans are much more expensive than standalone plans on offer externally. Always shop around, check for bargains and ensure the employer is giving you the best deal.

An edge that your company offers could be the fact that you will not need to be subjected to medical cross-examination to be enlisted on the scheme. Relying solely on your employers' life insurance could be a grotesque miscalculation that you could ever make.

Also in event that you leave the company, you will lose the employers insurance plan and you may have to re-qualify at an older age with a new provider or even be subjected to medical examination and increased premiums for the same amount of sum insured.

99. Disability Insurance.

This caters for a fraction of your monthly earnings in event of inability to work as a result of illness or injury. Some of the insurance coverage is quite costly and you could save some decent amount in dollars if you resolved to employers group plan as compared to individual plans.

Some employer disability insurance plans allow for conversion to individual plans upon leaving the company's employment.

100. Thinking is Hard Work

"Thinking is probably the hardest work there is, which is probably why so few engage in it"- **Henry Ford**

Ask those who have worked in a construction site, it's no mean feat! It will make you wake up to the realization that hard-work, value and money have no correlation. This is where thinking becomes just as important as hard work especially in building a financial future. Don't we know of people who have worked diligently and so hard in their whole lives yet they still ended up so broke?

As a matter of fact, building a financial future, whether it's that dream home, mobilizing savings or embarking on a sound investment that amounts to a flourishing life, is a matter of making calculated smart and dexterous decisions with reasonable hard work.

EPILOGUE

101. Learning from Adversity

> *"The best education we can ever receive is from the University of Adversity. It's the only institute of learning that rewards us when we fail."* **–Jason Versey**

Adversity could emanate from a business deal that has fallen through, grappling with pronounced financial hardships, end of the road in a relationship, pink-slipped from work or suffering from a critical illness. There never has been anyone in a respectable profession who rose to the highest level that hasn't undergone consequential setbacks in their lives or career.

When you anticipate adversity you won't get surprises on encountering it. The good news is that, when you persevere in the light of a rude awakening, disenchantment, disillusionment, disaffection, obstacles or a temporary defeat, the more powerful you become as a person.

With this kind of mindset, adversity becomes a hurdle to cross over rather than a ground to squelch. In his book *The Road Less Travelled*, M. Scott Peck begins the book with a powerful debut, "Life is difficult." The author intended adversity to be seen as an advancement opportunity to get ahead in terms of persistence and belief and cementing it until you eventually attain personal growth and become unstoppable.

It's for this reason that the best business moguls, gymnast, investors and other high performers do what is difficult, not easy. Otherwise these professions would have been littered with more people had it been easy to enter the race.

According to Napoleon Hill author of *Think & Grow Rich* in order to acquire immense wealth, the starting phase has to be the complete transformation of your mind so that you start by becoming financially frugal. Otherwise if it was all about hard work, he would have instead coined the title of the book to read, "Work hard and Grow Rich."

www.ingramcontent.com/pod-product-compliance
Lightning Source LLC
Chambersburg PA
CBHW021504210526
45463CB00002B/890